REEDS
MARINA GUIDE
2009

The source directory for all sail & power boat owners

© Adlard Coles Nautical 2008

Adlard Coles Nautical,
38 Soho Square, London W1D 3HB
Tel: 0207 758 0200
Fax: 0207 758 0222/0333
e-mail: info@reedsalmanac.co.uk
www.reedsalmanac.co.uk

Cover photo: Dean & Reddyhoff Ltd
Tel: 023 9260 1201
www.deanreddyhoff.co.uk

Section 1

The Marinas and Services Section has been fully updated for the 2009 season. These useful pages provide chartlets and facility details for some 175 marinas around the shores of the UK and Ireland, including the Channel Islands, the perfect complement to any *Reeds Nautical Almanac*.

Section 2

The Marine Supplies & Services section lists more than 500 services at coastal and other locations around the British Isles. It provides a quick and easy reference to manufacturers and retailers of equipment, services and supplies both nationally and locally together with emergency services.

Advertisement Sales

Enquiries about advertising space should be addressed to:

**MS Publications, 2nd Floor
Ewer House, 44-46 Crouch Street
Colchester, Essex, CO3 3HH
Tel: +44(0)1206 506227
Fax: +44 (0)1206 500228**

Section 1
Marinas and Services Section .....

Section 2
Marine Supplies and Services Section 133–160

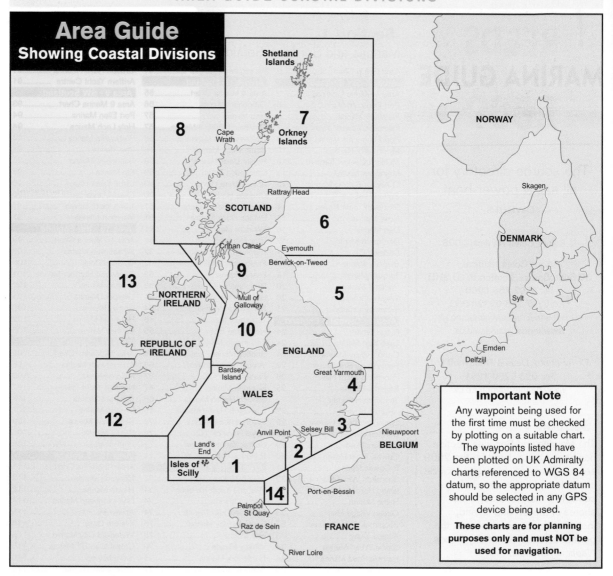

Area Guide
Showing Coastal Divisions

Important Note

Any waypoint being used for the first time must be checked by plotting on a suitable chart. The waypoints listed have been plotted on UK Admiralty charts referenced to WGS 84 datum, so the appropriate datum should be selected in any GPS device being used.

These charts are for planning purposes only and must NOT be used for navigation.

Area 1 ......**South West England**	....	Isles of Scilly to Anvil Point
Area 2 ......**Central Southern England**	....	Anvil Point to Selsey Bill
Area 3 ......**South East England**	....	Selsey Bill to North Foreland
Area 4 ......**East England**	....	North Foreland to Great Yarmouth
Area 5 ......**North East England**	....	Great Yarmouth to Berwick-upon-Tweed
Area 6 ......**South East Scotland**	....	Eyemouth to Rattray Head
Area 7 ......**North East Scotland**	....	Rattray Head to Cape Wrath including Orkney & Shetland Is
Area 8 ......**North West Scotland**	....	Cape Wrath to Crinan Canal
Area 9 .....**South West Scotland**	....	Crinan Canal to Mull of Galloway
Area 10 ....**North West England**	....	Isle of Man & N Wales, Mull of Galloway to Bardsey Is
Area 11 ....**South Wales & Bristol Channel**	....	Bardsey Island to Land's End
Area 12 ....**South Ireland**	....	Malahide, south to Liscanor Bay
Area 13 ....**North Ireland**	....	Lambay Island, north to Liscanor Bay
Area 14 ....**Channel Islands**	....	Guernsey, Jersey & Alderney

SOUTH WEST ENGLAND - Isles of Scilly to Anvil Point

Key to Marina Plans symbols

🛢	Bottled gas	P	Parking
	Chandler	✕	Pub/Restaurant
♿	Disabled facilities		Pump out
	Electrical supply		Rigging service
	Electrical repairs		Sail repairs
	Engine repairs	✕	Shipwright
✛	First Aid		Shop/Supermarket
	Fresh Water		Showers
D	Fuel - Diesel		Slipway
P	Fuel - Petrol	WC	Toilets
	Hardstanding/boatyard		Telephone
@	Internet Café		Trolleys
	Laundry facilities	V	Visitors berths
	Lift-out facilities		Wi-Fi

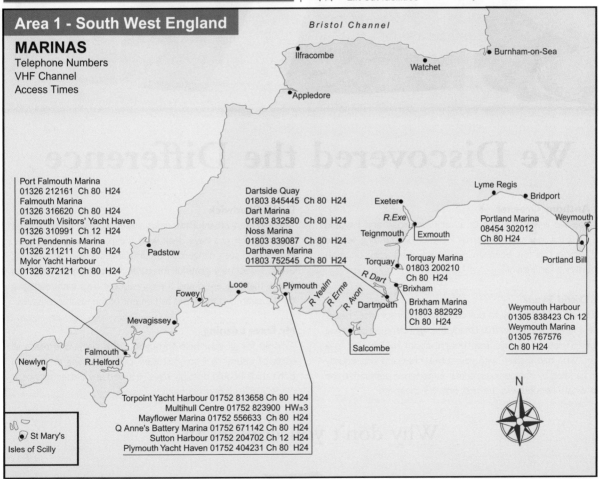

Area 1 - South West England

MARINAS
Telephone Numbers
VHF Channel
Access Times

Bristol Channel

• Ilfracombe
• Watchet
• Burnham-on-Sea

• Appledore

Port Falmouth Marina
01326 212161 Ch 80 H24
Falmouth Marina
01326 316620 Ch 80 H24
Falmouth Visitors' Yacht Haven
01326 310991 Ch 12 H24
Port Pendennis Marina
01326 211211 Ch 80 H24
Mylor Yacht Harbour
01326 372121 Ch 80 H24

Dartside Quay
01803 845445 Ch 80 H24
Dart Marina
01803 832580 Ch 80 H24
Noss Marina
01803 839087 Ch 80 H24
Darthaven Marina
01803 752545 Ch 80 H24

Lyme Regis
• Bridport
Exeter•
R.Exe
Teignmouth
Exmouth
Portland Marina
08454 302012
Ch 80 H24
Weymouth

Torquay• Torquay Marina
01803 200210
Ch 80 H24
Brixham•
Portland Bill

Padstow

Plymouth
R Yealm *R Erme* *R Avon* *R Dart*
Dartmouth
Brixham Marina
01803 882929
Ch 80 H24

Looe
Fowey

Mevagissey

Salcombe

Weymouth Harbour
01305 838423 Ch 12
Weymouth Marina
01305 767576
Ch 80 H24

Newlyn
Falmouth
R.Helford

St Mary's
Isles of Scilly

Torpoint Yacht Harbour 01752 813658 Ch 80 H24
Multihull Centre 01752 823900 HW±3
Mayflower Marina 01752 556633 Ch 80 H24
Q Anne's Battery Marina 01752 671142 Ch 80 H24
Sutton Harbour 01752 204702 Ch 12 H24
Plymouth Yacht Haven 01752 404231 Ch 80 H24

N

We Discovered the Difference

Sir Anthony Greener

"I hope we are at the end of a very long road and I would like to thank you and Pantaenius for your outstanding service and support. It has been an exemplary (and very unusual) experience for a client."

Mr. David Evans

"Why would I ever try to buy the cheapest insurance? I now have a self-satisfied glow that I made the right decision by buying the BEST insurance. This was brought about by listening to a friend who had a claim with yourselves. His claim was equally well handled by Pantaenius and that experience persuaded me that what I needed was the best, not the cheapest!"

Dr. H. Chadwick

"I would like to thank Pantaenius and especially yourself for the way in which you have dealt with things, as losing one's boat, especially in such dangerous circumstances is quite a traumatic event. I was very grateful for both the immediate help and advice that I received and the subsequent help with managing the situation and the rapid settlement of the insurance issues."

Mr. Dave Leaning

"Thanks for all your help throughout this claim, one reads all sorts of insurance horror stories in the yachting press but I don't think I could possibly have received any better service. It made a difficult process painless."

Why don't you contact us

2009/Mg9/v

PANTAENIUS
Yacht Insurance

Hamburg · Plymouth · Monaco · Skive · Vienna · Palma de Mallorca · Zagreb · New York

Marine Building · Victoria Wharf · Plymouth · Devon PL4 0RF · Phone +44-1752 22 36 56 · Fax +44-1752 22 36 37
Authorised and regulated by the Financial Services Authority

www.pantaenius.com

PORT FALMOUTH MARINA

Port Falmouth Marina
The Docks, Falmouth, TR11 4NR
Tel: 01326 212161 Fax: 01326 319433
Email: info@portfalmouth.com

VHF Ch 80
ACCESS H24

Port Falmouth Marina is an exciting new, world-class facility in the heart of Falmouth town.

The state-of-the-art 300-berth marina offers direct access to the sheltered waters of the Fal Estuary. A floating breakwater will protect the marina from prevailing winds and provide additional berthing for visitors and super-yachts. The inner pontoons will have finger berths to accommodate boats up to 18m LOA.

The marina plans include a drive on facility for the provisioning and servicing of yachts and high amp electricity outlets in addition to water and pump out facilities.

FACILITIES AT A GLANCE

FALMOUTH MARINA

Falmouth Marina
North Parade, Falmouth, Cornwall, TR11 2TD
Tel: 01326 316620 Fax: 01326 313939
Email: falmouth@premiermarinas.com
www.premiermarinas.com

VHF Ch 80
ACCESS H24

Falmouth Marina lies tucked away in sheltered waters at the southern end of the Fal Estuary. Welcoming to both visiting and residential yachts, its comprehensive

facilities include a restaurant, convenience store and hairdresser, while just a 20-minute walk away is Falmouth's town centre where you will find no shortage of shops and eating places. Comprising more than 70 sq miles of navigable water, the Fal Estuary is an intriguing cruising area full of hidden creeks and inlets.

FACILITIES AT A GLANCE

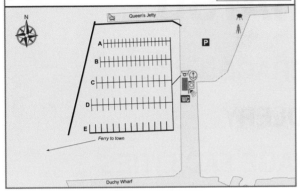

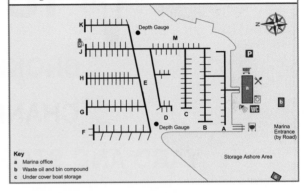

Key
a   Marina office
b   Waste oil and bin compound
c   Under cover boat storage

FALMOUTH VISITORS' YACHT HAVEN

Falmouth Visitors Yacht Haven
44 Arwenack Street
Tel: 01326 310991 Fax: 01326 211352
Email: admin@falmouthport.co.uk

VHF | Ch 12
ACCESS | H24

Run by Falmouth Harbour Commissioners (FHC), Falmouth Visitors' Yacht Haven has become increasingly popular since its opening in 1982, enjoying close proximity to the amenities and entertainments of Falmouth town centre. Sheltered by a breakwater, the Haven caters for 100 boats and offers petrol and diesel supplies as well as good shower and laundry facilities.

Falmouth Harbour is considered by some to be the cruising capital of Cornwall and its deep water combined with easily navigable entrance – even in the severest conditions – makes it a favoured destination for visiting yachtsmen.

FACILITIES AT A GLANCE

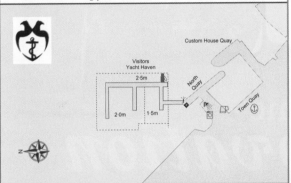

PORT PENDENNIS MARINA

Port Pendennis Marina
Challenger Quay, Falmouth, Cornwall, TR11 3YL
Tel: 01326 211211 Fax: 01326 311116
www.portpendennis.com

VHF | Ch 80
ACCESS | H24

Easily identified by the tower of the National Maritime Museum, Port Pendennis Marina is a convenient arrival or departure point for trans-Atlantic or Mediterranean voyages. Lying adjacent to the town centre, Port Pendennis is divided into an outer marina, with full tidal access, and inner marina, accessible three hours either side of HW. Among its impressive array of marine services is Pendennis Shipyard, one of Britain's most prestigious yacht builders, while other amenities on site include car hire, tennis courts and a yachtsman's lounge, from where you can send faxes or e-mails.

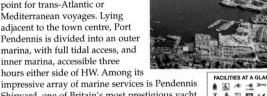

FACILITIES AT A GLANCE

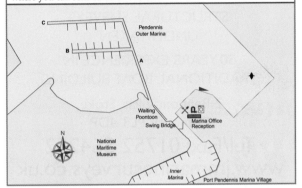

MYLOR YACHT HARBOUR

Mylor Yacht Harbour Marina
Mylor, Falmouth, Cornwall, TR11 5UF
Tel: 01326 372121 Fax: 01326 372120
Email: enquiries@mylor.com

VHF Ch M, 80
ACCESS H24

Situated on the western shore of Carrick Roads in the beautiful Fal Estuary, Mylor Yacht Harbour has been improved and expanded in recent years, now comprising two substantial breakwaters, three inner pontoons and approximately 250 moorings. With 24 hour access, good shelter and excellent facilities, it ranks among the most popular marinas on the SW Coast of England.

Formerly the Navy's smallest dockyard, established in 1805, Mylor is today a thriving yachting centre as well as home to the world's only remaining sailing oyster fishing fleet. With Falmouth just 10 mins away, local attractions include the Eden Project in St Austell and the National Maritime Museum in Falmouth.

FACILITIES AT A GLANCE

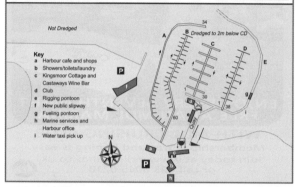

Key
a Harbour cafe and shops
b Showers/toilets/laundry
c Kingsmoor Cottage and Castaways Wine Bar
d Club
e Rigging pontoon
f New public slipway
g Fueling pontoon
h Marine services and Harbour office
i Water taxi pick up

MULTIHULL CENTRE, TORPOINT

Multihull Centre
Foss Quay, Millbrook, Torpoint, Cornwall, PL10 1EN
Tel: 01752 823900 Fax: 01752 823200
Email: info@multihullcentre.co.uk
www.multihullcentre.co.uk

VHF
ACCESS HW±3

Multihull Centre lies on the Cornish side of the River Tamar up the sheltered tidal inlet of Millbrook lake. The village of Millbrook has shops, pubs, fuel and public transport to Torpoint and Plymouth, the villages of Kingsand and Cawsand are less than 2 miles away. Mt Edgecumbe Country Park is close by.

The centre specialises in catamarans, trimarans, bilge keels and shoal draft craft. There are quay and pontoon berths and swinging moorings, all tidal (half tide). The Multihull Centre can provide moorings and storage ashore on its five acre site; facilities include a small chandlery, repairs, crane and lifting equipment.

FACILITIES AT A GLANCE

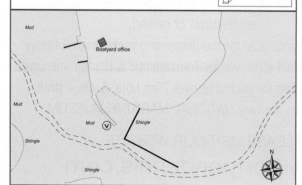

MAYFLOWER MARINA

Mayflower International Marina
Ocean Quay, Richmond Walk, Plymouth, PL1 4LS
Tel: 01752 556633 Fax: 01752 606896
Email: info@mayflowermarina.co.uk

VHF	Ch 80
ACCESS	H24

Sitting on the famous Plymouth Hoe, with the Devon coast to the left and the Cornish coast to the right, Mayflower Marina is a friendly, well-run marina. Facilities include 24 hour access to fuel, gas and a launderette, full repair and maintenance services as well as an on site bar and brasserie. The marina is located only a short distance from Plymouth's town centre, where there are regular train services to and from several major towns and cities.

FACILITIES AT A GLANCE

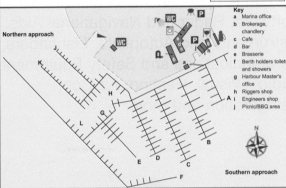

Northern approach

Southern approach

Key
a   Marina office
b   Brokerage, chandlery
c   Cafe
d   Bar
e   Brasserie
f   Berth holders toilets and showers
g   Harbour Master's office
h   Riggers shop
i   Engineers shop
j   Picnic/BBQ area

WAYPOINT 1
MARINE ELECTRONICS LTD

Main Agents for:
Raymarine, Simrad, Silva, Mcmurdo, Lowrance, Icom, Garmin, Mastervolt, CMap, Navionics, Webasto, Penguin, Frigoboat and many more.

We can supply and install Marine PC/ Software, Radar and Navigational Aids, Instruments and Autopilots, Fishfinders, Communications and Safety Equipment, Audio - Visual, Heating, Air Con, Refrigeration and more.

Your first port of call for Marine Electronics

Ocean Building,
Queen Anne's Battery,
Plymouth, Devon, PL4 0LP
Tel 01752 661913 Fax 01752 661931
enquiries@waypoint-1.co.uk

Shop on-line at
www.waypoint-1.co.uk

2009/MG51/z

QUEEN ANNE'S BATTERY MARINA

Queen Anne's Battery
Plymouth, PL4 0LP
Tel: 01752 671142 Fax: 01752 266297
www.marinas.co.uk Email: qab@mdlmarinas.co.uk

VHF	Ch 80
ACCESS	H24

At the centre of Plymouth lies Queen Anne's Battery, comprising 280 resident berths as well as a visitor's basin with alongside pontoon berthing. All berths are well protected by a breakwater and double wavescreen.

As Plymouth Sound frequently provides the starting point for many prestigious international yacht races as well as the finish of the Fastnet Race, the marina is often crowded with racers during the height of the season and its vibrant atmosphere can at times resemble a mini 'Cowes'.

FACILITIES AT A GLANCE

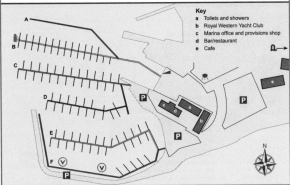

Key
a Toilets and showers
b Royal Western Yacht Club
c Marina office and provisions shop
d Bar/restaurant
e Cafe

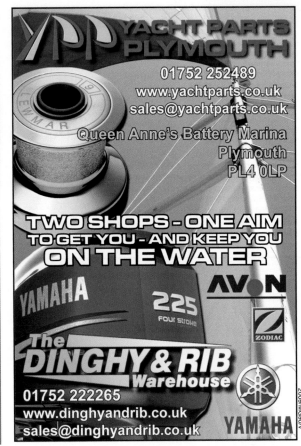

SUTTON HARBOUR

Sutton Harbour
The Jetty, Sutton Harbour, Plymouth, PL4 0DW
Tel: 01752 204702 Fax: 01752 204693
Email: marina@sutton-harbour.co.uk
www.sutton-harbour.co.uk

VHF	Ch 12
ACCESS	H24

Boasting a superb location alongside Plymouth's famous Barbican centre, Sutton Harbour lies just north of Queen Anne's Battery Marina. The harbour can be entered 24 hours a day via a lock which is marked by green and red chevrons. Affording good shelter in 3.5m of water, it offers a comprehensive range of marine services, including a fuel berth that opens from 0800 to 1800.

Situated within a minute's walk from the marina is a Tourist Information Centre, providing all the necessary details of how best to explore the surrounding Devon countryside.

FACILITIES AT A GLANCE

Key
a Fish market
b National Marine Aquarium
c Customs House
d The Cove
e Marina office
f Lock tower

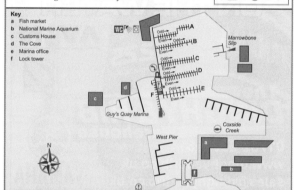

PLYMOUTH YACHT HAVEN

Plymouth Yacht Haven Ltd
Shaw Way, Mount Batten, Plymouth, PL9 9XH
Tel: 01752 404231 Fax: 01752 484177
www.yachthavens.com Email: plymouth@yachthavens.com

VHF	Ch 80
ACCESS	H24

Situated at the mouth of the river Plym, Plymouth Yacht Haven offers good protection from the prevailing winds and is within close proximity of Plymouth Sound. This 450 berth marina can accommodate vessels up to 45m in length and 7m draught. Members of staff are on site 24/7 to welcome you as a visitor and to serve diesel. 2008 sees the opening of a brand new bar and restaurant at the heart of the marina. Within easy access are coastal walks, a golf course, and health centre with heated swimming pool. The city of Plymouth and historic Barbican are a short water-taxi ride away.

With a 65ton travel hoist, undercover storage, and extensive range of marine services onsite, Plymouth Yacht Haven has the perfect yard for

FACILITIES AT A GLANCE

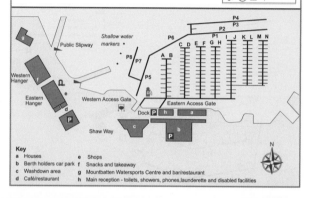

Key
a Houses
b Berth holders car park
c Washdown area
d Café/restaurant
e Shops
f Snacks and takeaway
g Mountbatten Watersports Centre and bar/restaurant
h Main reception - toilets, showers, phones, launderette and disabled facilities

NOSS MARINA

Noss Marina
Bridge Road, Kingswear, Devon, TQ6 0EA
Tel: 01803 839087 Fax: 01803 835620
Email: info@nossmarina.com
www.nossmarina.com

VHF	Ch 80
ACCESS	H24

Upstream of Dartmouth on the east shore of the River Dart is Noss Marina. Enjoying a peaceful rural setting, this marina is well suited to those who prefer a quieter atmosphere. Besides 180 fully serviced berths, 50 fore-and-aft moorings in the middle reaches of the river are also run by the marina, with mooring holders entitled to use all the facilities available to berth holders. During summer, a passenger ferry service runs regularly between Noss-on-Dart and Dartmouth, while a grocery service to your boat can be provided on request.

FACILITIES AT A GLANCE

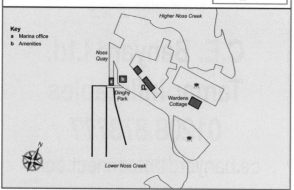

Key
a Marina office
b Amenities

Higher Noss Creek

Noss Quay

Dinghy Park

Wardens Cottage

Lower Noss Creek

DART MARINA

Dart Marina
Sandquay Road, Dartmouth
Devon, TQ6 9PH
Tel: 01803 832580 Fax: 01803 835040
Email: yachtharbour@dartmarina.com www.dartmarina.com

VHF	Ch 80
ACCESS	H24

Annual berth holders enjoy the finest marina location in the West Country, with the atmosphere and facilities of an exclusive club. The Yacht Harbour on the River Dart is a perfect retreat for simply relaxing and an ideal base for local boating and more ambitious cruising further afield. During the season there are a limited number of visitors' berths available and a waiting list for the 110 annual berths. The berths are accessible at any tide and are located in peaceful surroundings, just a short walk along the riverfront from Dartmouth's historic centre.

The showers and bathrooms are of high quality and some first class facilities are conveniently onsite - the Wildfire Bistro, Health Spa, River Restaurant and quayside dining.

FACILITIES AT A GLANCE

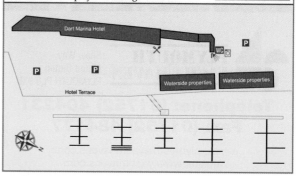

Dart Marina Hotel

Waterside properties   Waterside properties

Hotel Terrace

DARTHAVEN MARINA

Darthaven Marina
Brixham Road, Kingswear, Devon, TQ6 0SG
Tel: 01803 752545 Fax: 01803 752722
Email: darthaven@darthaven.co.uk
www.darthaven.co.uk

| VHF | Ch 80 |
| ACCESS | H24 |

Darthaven Marina is a family run business situated in the village of Kingswear on the east side of the River Dart. Within half a mile from Start Bay and the mouth of the river, it is the first marina you come to from seaward and is accessible at all states of the tide. Darthaven prides itself on being more than just a marina, offering a high standard of marine services with both electronic and engineering experts plus wood and GRP repairs on site. A shop, post office and five pubs are within a walking distance of the marina, while a frequent ferry service takes passengers across the river to Dartmouth.

FACILITIES AT A GLANCE

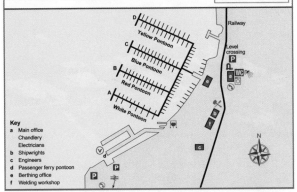

Key
a   Main office
      Chandlery
      Electricians
b   Shipwrights
c   Engineers
d   Passenger ferry pontoon
e   Berthing office
f   Welding workshop

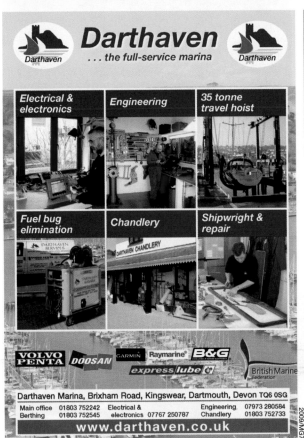

DARTSIDE QUAY

Dartside Quay
Galmpton Creek, Brixham, Devon, TQ5 0EH
Tel: 01803 845445 Fax: 01803 843558
Email: dartsidequay@mdlmarinas.co.uk

| VHF | Ch 80 |
| ACCESS | H24 |

Located at the head of Galmpton Creek, Dartside Quay lies three miles up river from Dartmouth.
    In a sheltered position and with beautiful views across to Dittisham, it offers extensive boatyard facilities. The 7-acre dry boat storage area has space for over 300 boats and is serviced by a 65-ton hoist operating from a purpose-built dock, a 16-ton trailer hoist and 25-ton crane.
    There are also a number of summer mud moorings available and a well stocked chandlery, in fact if the item you want is not in stock we can order it in for you.

FACILITIES AT A GLANCE

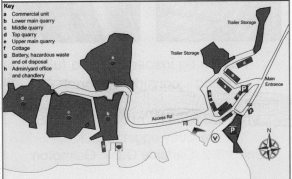

Key
a   Commercial unit
b   Lower main quarry
c   Middle quarry
d   Top quarry
e   Upper main quarry
f   Cottage
g   Battery, hazardous waste
      and oil disposal
h   Admin/yard office
      and chandlery

Trailer Storage

Trailer Storage

Main Entrance

Access Rd

2009/MG7/e

BRIXHAM MARINA

Brixham Marina
Berry Head Road, Brixham
Devon, TQ5 9BW
Tel: 01803 882929 Fax: 01803 882737
www.marinas.co.uk Email: brixham@mdlmarinas.co.uk

VHF	Ch 80
ACCESS	H24

Home to one of Britain's largest fishing fleets, Brixham Harbour is located on the southern shore of Tor Bay, which is well sheltered from westerly winds and where tidal streams are weak. Brixham Marina, housed in a separate basin to the work boats, provides easy access in all weather conditions and at all states of the tide. Established in 1989, it has become increasingly popular with locals and visitors alike, enjoying an idyllic setting right on the town's quayside.

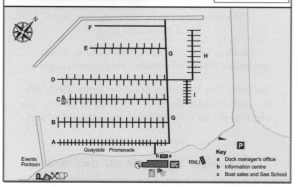

Local attractions include a walk out to Berry Head Nature Reserve and a visit to the replica of Sir Francis Drake's ship, the *Golden Hind*.

FACILITIES AT A GLANCE

Key
a   Dock manager's office
b   Information centre
c   Boat sales and Sea School

Events Pontoon
Quayside Promenade
RNLI

TORQUAY MARINA

Torquay Marina
Torquay, Devon, TQ2 5EQ
Tel: 01803 200210 Fax: 01803 200225
Emails: torquaymarina@mdlmarinas.co.uk

VHF Ch 80
ACCESS H24

Tucked away in the north east corner of Tor Bay, Torquay Marina is well sheltered from the prevailing SW'ly winds, providing safe entry in all conditions and at any state of the tide. Located in the centre of Torquay, the marina enjoys easy access to the town's numerous shops, bars and restaurants.

On the starboard hand near the harbour entrance is the borough council-owned Town Dock with limited visitor berths.

Torquay is ideally situated for either exploring Tor Bay itself, with its many delightful anchorages, or else for heading further west to experience several other scenic harbours such as Dartmouth and Salcombe. It also provides a good starting point for crossing to Brittany, Normandy or the Channel Islands.

FACILITIES AT A GLANCE

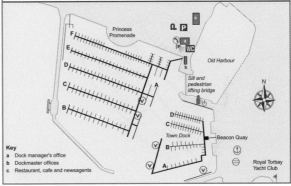

Key
a Dock manager's office
b Dockmaster offices
c Restaurant, cafe and newsagents

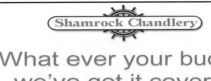

PORTLAND MARINA

Portland Marina
Osprey Quay, Portland, Dorset, DT5 1DX
Tel: 08454 302012 Fax: 08451 802012
www.deanreddyhoff.co.uk
Email: sales@portlandmarina.co.uk

VHF	Ch 80
ACCESS	H24

Brand new for 2009, Portland Marina is an ideal location for both year-round berthing and weekend stopovers. The marina offers first class facilities including the highest quality washrooms, on-site bar and restaurant, sewage pump out, lift out up to 320t and storage, dry stack up to 10m, marine engineering, chandlery and rigging services, to name but a few, and 24-hour on-site security and CCTV. The 600 berth marina officially opens on 1 April 2009 but at the time of writing (July 2008) it has not been confirmed that the fuel berth will be open for the 2009 season so it is best to call ahead.

In the Olympic context, preparations are well advanced. The adjacent National Sailing Academy, a focal point for the Olympics, works closely with the marina to provide additional facilities on reclaimed land and berths for keelboats in the lee of a second rock breakwater.

FACILITIES AT A GLANCE

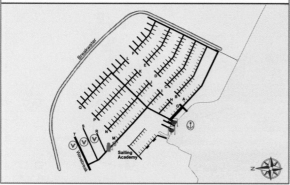

WEYMOUTH MARINA

Weymouth Marina
70 Commercial Road, Dorset, DT4 8NA
Tel: 01305 767576 Fax: 01305 767575
www.weymouth-marina.co.uk
Email: sales@weymouth-marina.co.uk

VHF	Ch 80
ACCESS	H24

With more than 280 permanent and visitors' berths, Weymouth is a modern, purpose-built marina ideally situated for yachtsmen cruising between the West Country and the Solent. It is also conveniently placed for sailing to France or the Channel Islands.

Accessed via the town's historic lifting bridge, which opens every even hour 0800–2000 (plus 2100 Jun–Aug), the marina is dredged to 2.5m below chart datum. It provides easy access to the town centre, with its abundance of shops, pubs and restaurants, as well as to the traditional seafront where an impressive sandy beach is overlooked by an esplanade of hotels. More details can be found at www.weymouthmarina.co.uk.

FACILITIES AT A GLANCE

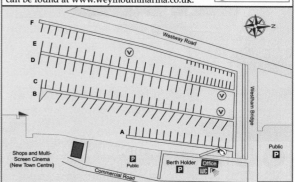

WEYMOUTH HARBOUR

Weymouth & Portland Borough Council
North Quay, Weymouth, Dorset, DT4 8TA
Tel: 01305 838423 Fax: 01305 767927
Email: berthingoffice@weymouth.gov.uk

VHF Ch 12
ACCESS H24

Weymouth Harbour, which lies to the NE of Portland in the protected waters of Weymouth Bay, benefits from deep water at all states of the tide. If wishing to moor in the old Georgian outer harbour, you should contact the harbour authority, which also controls several municipal pontoons above the bridge. In recent years the facilities have been improved and now include electricity and fresh water on both quays, as well as free showers and a coin-operated launderette. Visiting yachtsmen are very welcome both at the Royal Dorset Yacht Club, situated on Customs House Quay in the inner harbour, and the Weymouth Sailing Club, on the south pier of the outer harbour.

FACILITIES AT A GLANCE

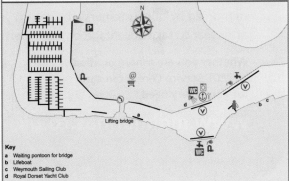

Key
a Waiting pontoon for bridge
b Lifeboat
c Weymouth Sailing Club
d Royal Dorset Yacht Club

CENTRAL SOUTHERN ENGLAND - Anvil Point to Selsey Bill

ADLARD COLES NAUTICAL
WEATHER FORECASTS
BY FAX & TELEPHONE

Coastal/Inshore	2-day by Fax	5-day by Phone
South West	09065 222 348	09068 969 648
Mid Channel	09065 222 347	09068 969 647
Channel East	09065 222 346	09068 969 646
NE France	09065 501 611	09064 700 421
N France	09065 501 612	09064 700 422
N Brittany	09065 501 613	09064 700 423

Offshore	2-5 day by Fax	2-5 day by Phone
English Channel	09065 222 357	09068 969 657
Southern North Sea	09065 222 358	09068 969 658
Biscay	09065 222 360	09068 969 660

09064/68 CALLS COST 60P PER MIN. 09065 CALLS COST £1.50 PER MIN.

Key to Marina Plans symbols

Bottled gas		Parking
Chandler		Pub/Restaurant
Disabled facilities		Pump out
Electrical supply		Rigging service
Electrical repairs		Sail repairs
Engine repairs		Shipwright
First Aid		Shop/Supermarket
Fresh Water		Showers
Fuel - Diesel		Slipway
Fuel - Petrol		Toilets
Hardstanding/boatyard		Telephone
Internet Café		Trolleys
Laundry facilities		Visitors berths
Lift-out facilities		Wi-Fi

Area 2 - Central Southern England

MARINAS
Telephone Numbers
VHF Channel
Access Times

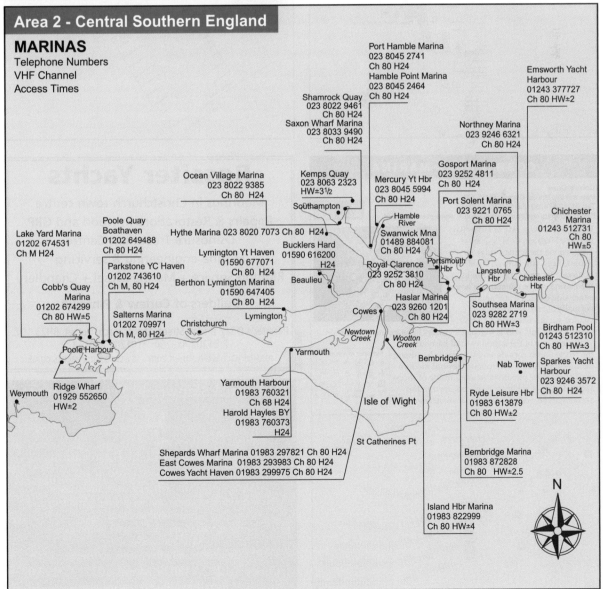

Port Hamble Marina 023 8045 2741 Ch 80 H24
Hamble Point Marina 023 8045 2464 Ch 80 H24
Emsworth Yacht Harbour 01243 377727 Ch 80 HW±2
Shamrock Quay 023 8022 9461 Ch 80 H24
Saxon Wharf Marina 023 8033 9490 Ch 80 H24
Northney Marina 023 9246 6321 Ch 80 H24
Ocean Village Marina 023 8022 9385 Ch 80 H24
Kemps Quay 023 8063 2323 HW±3½
Gosport Marina 023 9252 4811 Ch 80 H24
Mercury Yt Hbr 023 8045 5994 Ch 80 H24
Port Solent Marina 023 9221 0765 Ch 80 H24
Chichester Marina 01243 512731 Ch 80 HW±5
Southampton
Hamble River
Lake Yard Marina 01202 674531 Ch M H24
Poole Quay Boathaven 01202 649488 Ch 80 H24
Hythe Marina 023 8020 7073 Ch 80 H24
Bucklers Hard 01590 616200 H24
Swanwick Mna 01489 884081 Ch 80 H24
Portsmouth Hbr
Langstone Hbr
Chichester Hbr
Lymington Yt Haven 01590 677071 Ch 80 H24
Royal Clarence 023 9252 3810
Parkstone YC Haven 01202 743610 Ch M, 80 H24
Beaulieu
Cobb's Quay Marina 01202 674299 Ch 80 HW±5
Berthon Lymington Marina 01590 647405 Ch 80 H24
Haslar Marina 023 9260 1201 Ch 80 H24
Southsea Marina 023 9282 2719 Ch 80 HW±3
Salterns Marina 01202 709971 Ch M, 80 H24
Christchurch
Lymington
Cowes
Birdham Pool 01243 512310 Ch 80 HW±3
Poole Harbour
Newtown Creek
Wootton Creek
Bembridge
Nab Tower
Sparkes Yacht Harbour 023 9246 3572 Ch 80 H24
Weymouth
Ridge Wharf 01929 552650 HW±2
Yarmouth
Yarmouth Harbour 01983 760321 Ch 68 H24
Harold Hayles BY 01983 760373 H24
Isle of Wight
Ryde Leisure Hbr 01983 613879 Ch 80 HW±2
St Catherines Pt
Shepards Wharf Marina 01983 297821 Ch 80 H24
East Cowes Marina 01983 293983 Ch 80 H24
Cowes Yacht Haven 01983 299975 Ch 80 H24
Bembridge Marina 01983 872828 Ch 80 HW±2.5
Island Hbr Marina 01983 822999 Ch 80 HW±4
N

RIDGE WHARF YACHT CENTRE

Ridge Wharf Yacht Centre
Ridge, Wareham, Dorset, BH20 5BG
Tel: 01929 552650 Fax: 01929 554434
Email: office@ridgewharf.co.uk

VHF
ACCESS HW±2

On the south bank of the River Frome, which acts as the boundary to the North of the Isle of Purbeck, is Ridge Wharf Yacht Centre. Access for a 1.5m draught is between one and two hours either side of HW, with berths drying out to soft mud. The Yacht Centre cannot be contacted on VHF, so it is best to phone up ahead of time to inquire about berthing availability.

A trip upstream to the ancient market town of Wareham is well worth while, although owners of deep-draughted yachts may prefer to go by dinghy. Tucked between the Rivers Frome and Trent, it is packed full of cafés, restaurants and shops.

FACILITIES AT A GLANCE

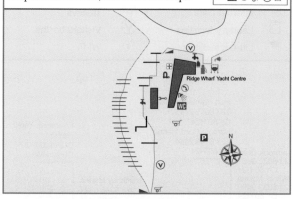

LAKE YARD MARINA

Lake Yard Marina
Lake Drive, Hamworthy, Poole, Dorset BH15 4DT
Tel: 01202 674531 Fax: 01202 677518
Email: office@lakeyard.com www.lakeyard.com

VHF Ch M
ACCESS H24

Lake Yard is situated towards the NW end of Poole Harbour, just beyond the SHM No 73. The entrance can be easily identified by 2FR (vert) and 2FG (vert) lights. Enjoying 24 hour access, the marina has no designated visitors' berths, but will accommodate visiting yachtsmen if resident berth holders are away. Its on site facilities include full maintenance and repair services as well as hard standing and a 50 ton boat hoist, although for the nearest fuel go to Corralls (Tel 01202 674551), opposite the Town Quay. Lake Yard's Waterfront Club, offering spectacular views across the harbour, opens seven days a week for lunchtime and evening meals.

FACILITIES AT A GLANCE

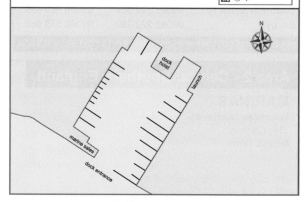

COBB'S QUAY MARINA

Cobb's Quay
Hamworthy, Poole, Dorset, BH15 4EL
Tel: 01202 674299 Fax: 01202 665217
Email: cobbsquay@mdlmarinas.co.uk www.marinas.co.uk

VHF Ch 80
ACCESS HW±5

Lying on the west side of Holes Bay in Poole Harbour, Cobb's Quay is accessed via the lifting bridge at Poole Quay. With fully serviced pontoons for yachts up to 25m LOA, the marina can be entered five hours either side of high water and is normally able to accommodate visiting yachts. On site is Cobb's Quay Yacht Club, which welcomes visitors to its bar and restaurant.

Poole is one of the largest natural harbours in the world and is considered by many to be among the finest. Its N side incorporates several modern marinas in close proximity to a multitude of shops and restaurants, while its S side boasts tranquil anchorages set within unspoilt nature reserves.

FACILITIES AT A GLANCE

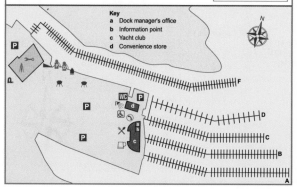

2

POOLE QUAY BOAT HAVEN

Poole Quay Boat Haven
Poole Town Quay, Poole, Dorset, BH15 1BT
Tel: 01202 649488 Fax: 01202 649488
Email: poolequayboathaven@phc.co.uk

VHF	Ch 80
ACCESS	H24

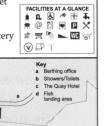

Once inside the Poole Harbour entrance small yachts heading for Poole Quay Boat Haven should use the Boat Channel running parallel south of the dredged Middle Ship Channel, which is primarily used by ferries sailing to and from the Hamworthy terminal. The marina can be accessed via the Little Channel and is easily identified by the large breakwater alongside the Quay. With deep water at all states of the tide the marina has berthing available for 125 yachts up to 30m, but due to its central location the marina can get busy so it is best to reserve a berth.

There is easy access to all of Poole Quay's facilities including restaurants, bars, Poole Pottery and the Waterfront Museum.

FACILITIES AT A GLANCE

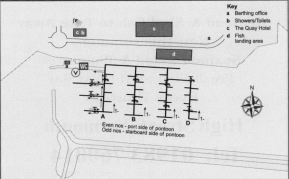

Key
a Berthing office
b Showers/Toilets
c The Quay Hotel
d Fish landing area

A B C D
Even nos - port side of pontoon
Odd nos - starboard side of pontoon
N

PARKSTONE YACHT CLUB HAVEN

Parkstone Yacht Club
Pearce Avenue, Parkstone, Poole, Dorset, BH14 8EH
Tel: 01202 743610 Fax: 01202 716394
Email: haven@parkstoneyachtclub.co.uk

VHF	Ch M, 80
ACCESS	H24

Situated on the north side of Poole Harbour between Salterns Marina and Poole Quay Boat Haven, Parkstone Yacht Club Haven can be entered at all states of the tides. Its approach channel has been dredged to 2.0m and is clearly marked by buoys. Run by the Parkstone Yacht Club, the Haven provides 200 deep water berths for members and visitors' berths. Other facilities include a bar, restaurant, new shower/changing rooms and wi-fi. With a busy sailing programme for over 2,500 members, the Yacht Club plays host to a variety of events including Poole Week, which is held towards the end of August.

FACILITIES AT A GLANCE

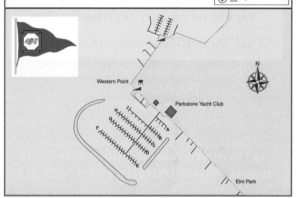

SALTERNS MARINA

Salterns Marina
40 Salterns Way, Lilliput, Poole
Dorset, BH14 8JR
Tel: 01202 709971 Fax: 01202 700398
Email: marina@salterns.co.uk www.salterns.co.uk

VHF	Ch M, 80
ACCESS	H24

Holding both the Blue Flag and Five Gold Anchor awards, Salterns Marina provides a service which is second to none. Located off the North Channel, it is approached from the No 31 SHM and benefits from deep water at all states of the tide. Facilities include 220 alongside pontoon berths as well as 75 swinging moorings with a free launch service. However, with very few designated visitors' berths, it is best to contact the marina ahead of time for availability. Fuel, diesel and gas can all be obtained 24 hours a day and the well-stocked chandlery, incorporating a coffee shop, stays open seven days a week.

FACILITIES AT A GLANCE

Key
a Marina office
  Reception
  Chandlery
  Salterns Brokerage
  Coffee shop
  Toilets/Showers
  Marine Sales
  Laundry

Sales Offices:
  Princess
  Golden Arrow Electronics
  Nordic Marine
  Wessex Marine
  Poole Aquatic Ltd
  North Haven
  Crest Marine

b Fuel pumps
  Yacht hoist
c Crest Marine
d Dinghy racks
e Toilets & showers
f Salterns Hotel
g Boatyard workshop
h 45 tonne travel hoist
i Boatyard office
  Engine & boat sales

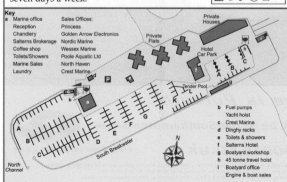

YARMOUTH HBR/HAROLD HAYLES BY

Yarmouth Harbour
Yarmouth, Isle of Wight, PO41 0NT
Tel: 01983 760321 Fax: 01983 761192
info@yarmouth-harbour.co.uk
www.yarmouth-harbour.co.uk

| VHF | Ch 68 |
| ACCESS | H24 |

Harold Hayles Ltd
The Quay, Yarmouth, Isle of Wight, PO41 0RS
Tel: 01983 760373 Fax: 01983 760666
Email: info@spurscutters.co.uk
www.spurscutters.co.uk

| VHF | |
| ACCESS | H24 |

The most western harbour on the Isle of Wight, Yarmouth is not only a convenient passage stopover but has become a very desirable destination in its own right, with virtually all weather and tidal access, although strong N to NE'ly winds can produce a considerable swell. The HM launch patrols the harbour entrance and will direct visiting yachtsmen to a pontoon berth or pile. The pretty harbour and town offer plenty of fine restaurants and amenities.

Walkashore pontoon moorings are available from the local boatyard, Harold Hayles Ltd, in the SW corner of the harbour. Pre-booking is preferred for both individuals or rallies.

FACILITIES AT A GLANCE

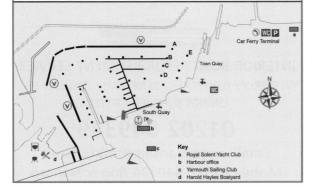

Key
a Royal Solent Yacht Club
b Harbour office
c Yarmouth Sailing Club
d Harold Hayles Boatyard

LYMINGTON YACHT HAVEN

Lymington Yacht Haven
King's Saltern Road, Lymington, S041 3QD
Tel: 01590 677071 Fax: 01590 678186
Email: lymington@yachthavens.com www.yachthavens.com

VHF **Ch 80**
ACCESS **H24**

The attractive old market town of Lymington lies at the western end of the Solent, just three miles from the Needles Channel. Despite the numerous ferries plying to and from the Isle of Wight, the river is well sheltered and navigable at all states of the tide, proving a popular destination with visiting yachtsmen. LPG is available.

Lymington Yacht Haven is the first of the two marinas from seaward, situated on the port hand side. Offering easy access to the Solent, it is a 10-minute walk to the town centre and supermarkets.

FACILITIES AT A GLANCE

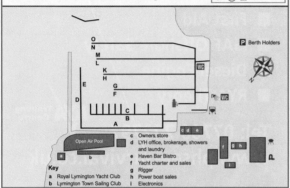

Key
a Royal Lymington Yacht Club
b Lymington Town Sailng Club

c Owners store
d LYH office, brokerage, showers and laundry
e Haven Bar Bistro
f Yacht charter and sales
g Rigger
h Power boat sales
i Electronics

BERTHON LYMINGTON MARINA

Berthon Lymington Marina Ltd
The Shipyard, Lymington, Hampshire, SO41 3YL
Tel: 01590 647405 Fax: 01590 676353
www.berthon.co.uk Email: marina@berthon.co.uk

VHF Ch 80
ACCESS H24

Situated approximately half a mile up river of Lymington Yacht Haven, on the port hand side, is Lymington Marina. Easily accessible at all states of the tide, it offers between 60 to 70 visitors' berths, although its close proximity to the town centre and first rate services mean that it can get very crowded in summer.

Besides the numerous attractions and activities to be found in the town itself, Lymington also benefits from having the New Forest, with its wild ponies and picturesque scenery, literally on its doorstep. Alternatively, the Solent Way footpath provides an invigorating walk to and from Hurst Castle.

FACILITIES AT A GLANCE

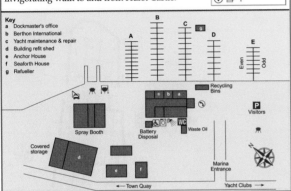

Key
a Dockmaster's office
b Berthon International
c Yacht maintenance & repair
d Building refit shed
e Anchor House
f Seaforth House
g Refueller

BUCKLERS HARD MARINA

Bucklers Hard
Beaulieu, Brockenhurst, Hampshire, SO42 7XB
Tel: 01590 616200 Fax: 01590 616211
www.bucklershard.co.uk Email: river@beaulieu.co.uk

VHF
ACCESS H24

Meandering through the New Forest, the Beaulieu River is considered by many to be one of the most attractive harbours on the mainland side of the Solent. Two miles upstream from the mouth of the river lies Bucklers Hard, an historic 18th century village where shipwrights skilfully constructed warships for Nelson's fleet. The Maritime Museum, showing the history of boat-building in the village, is open throughout the year.

The marina is manned 24/7 and offers deep water to visitors at all states of the tide, although the bar at the river's entrance should be avoided two hours either side of LW.

FACILITIES AT A GLANCE

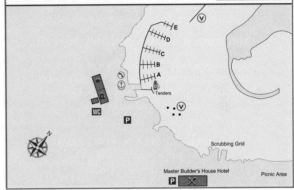

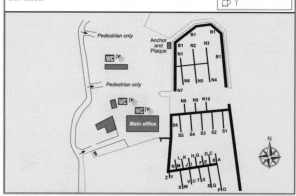

EAST COWES MARINA

East Cowes Marina
Britannia Way, East Cowes, Isle of Wight, PO32 6UB
Tel: 01983 293983 Fax: 01983 299276
www.eastcowesmarina.co.uk
Email: miket@eastcowesmarina.co.uk

VHF Ch 80
ACCESS H24

Accommodating around 230 residential yachts and 160 visiting boats, East Cowes Marina is situated on the quiet and protected east bank of the Medina River, about a quarter mile above the chain ferry. The on-site chandlery stocks essential marine equipment and a small convenience store is just five minutes walk away. The brand new *club style* centrally heated shower and toilet facilities ensure the visitor a warm welcome at any time of the year, as does the on-site bar and restaurant.

Several water taxis provide a return service to Cowes, ensuring a quick and easy way of getting to the town centre.

FACILITIES AT A GLANCE

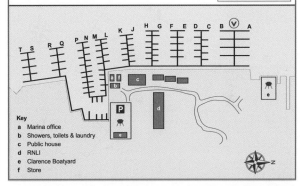

Key
a   Marina office
b   Showers, toilets & laundry
c   Public house
d   RNLI
e   Clarence Boatyard
f   Store

SHEPARDS WHARF MARINA

Shepards Wharf Boatyard
Medina Road, Cowes, Isle of Wight, PO31 7HT
Tel: 01983 297821 Fax: 01983 294814
www.shephards.co.uk

VHF Ch 80
ACCESS H24

A cable upstream of Cowes Yacht Haven, still on the starboard side, is Shepards Wharf. Incorporating several visitor pontoon berths, its facilities include water as well as full boatyard services ranging from a chandler and sailmaker to a 20-ton boat hoist. Fuel can be obtained from Lallows Boatyard (Tel 01983 292111) or Cowes Yacht Haven. For berthing availability, visiting yachtsmen should contact Cowes Harbour Control on VHF Ch 69 or Tel 01983 293952.

Shepards Wharf is within easy walking distance of Cowes town centre, where among the restaurants to be highly recommended are the Red Duster and Murrays Seafoods on the High Street and Tonino's on Shooters Hill. Also worth visiting are the Maritime Museum, exhibiting the Uffa Fox boats *Avenger* and *Coweslip*, and the Sir Max Aitken Museum. Sir Max contributed enormously to ocean yacht racing and the museum is dedicated to his collection of nautical instruments, paintings and maritime artefacts.

FACILITIES AT A GLANCE

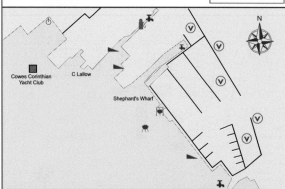

ISLAND HARBOUR MARINA

Island Harbour Marina
Mill Lane, Binfield, Newport, Isle of Wight, PO30 2LA
Tel: 01983 822999 Fax: 01983 526020
Email: info@island-harbour.co.uk

VHF Ch 80
ACCESS HW±4

Situated in beautiful rolling farmland about half a mile south of Folly Inn, Island Harbour Marina provides around 200 visitors' berths. Protected by a lock that is operated daily from 0700 – 2100 during the summer and from 0800 – 1730 during the winter, the marina is accessible for about four hours either side of HW for draughts of 1.5m.

Due to its remote setting, the marina's on site restaurant also sells essential provisions and newspapers. A half hour walk along the river brings you to Newport, the capital and county town of the Isle of Wight.

FACILITIES AT A GLANCE

Key
a Control tower
b Bin store
c Chandlery
d Restaurant

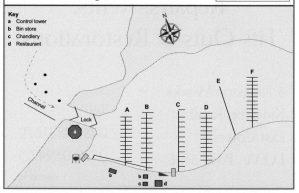

HYTHE MARINA

Hythe Marina Village
Shamrock Way, Hythe, Southampton, SO45 6DY
Tel: 023 8020 7073 Fax: 023 8084 2424
www.marinas.co.uk Email: d.wilson@mdlmarinas.co.uk

VHF Ch 80
ACCESS H24

Situated on the western shores of Southampton Water, Hythe Marina Village is approached by a dredged channel leading to a lock basin. The lock gates are controlled 24 hours a day throughout the year, with a waiting pontoon to the south of the approach basin.

Hythe Marina Village incorporates full marine services as well as on site restaurants and shops. Forming an integral part of the New Forest Waterside, Hythe is the perfect base from which to explore Hampshire's pretty inland villages and towns, or alternatively you can catch the ferry to Southampton's Town Quay.

FACILITIES AT A GLANCE

Key
a Salt Bar and Kitchen
b Lock building
c Boat storage and Trailer park

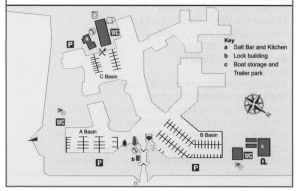

2

OCEAN VILLAGE MARINA

Ocean Village Marina
2 Channel Way, Southampton, SO14 3TG
Tel: 023 8022 9385 Fax: 023 8023 3515
www.marinas.co.uk Email: oceanvillage@mdlmarinas.co.uk

VHF Ch 80
ACCESS H24

The entrance to Ocean Village Marina lies on the port side of the River Itchen, just before the Itchen Bridge. With the capacity to accommodate large yachts and tall ships, the marina, accessible 24 hours a day, is renowned for hosting the starts of the Volvo and BT Global Challenge races. Situated at the heart of a waterside development incorporating shops, cinemas, restaurants and housing as well as The Royal Southampton Yacht Club, Ocean Village offers a vibrant atmosphere along with high quality service.

FACILITIES AT A GLANCE

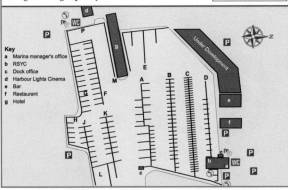

Key
a Marina manager's office
b RSYC
c Dock office
d Harbour Lights Cinema
e Bar
f Restaurant
g Hotel

SHAMROCK QUAY MARINA

Shamrock Quay Marina
William Street, Northam, Southampton, Hants, SO14 5QL
Tel: 023 8022 9461 Fax: 023 8021 3808
Email: shamrockquay@mdlmarinas.co.uk

VHF Ch 80
ACCESS H24

Shamrock Quay, lying upstream of the Itchen Bridge on the port hand side, offers excellent facilities to yachtsmen. It also benefits from being accessible 24 hours a day, although the inside berths can get quite shallow at LWS. Note that it is best to arrive at slack water as the cross tide can be tricky when close quarter manoeuvring.

The city centre is about two miles away, where among the numerous attractions are the Maritime Museum at Town Quay, the Medieval Merchant's House in French Street and the Southampton City Art Gallery in the Civic Centre.

FACILITIES AT A GLANCE

Key
a Ofice, bar and restaurant
b Marina office
c Cafe

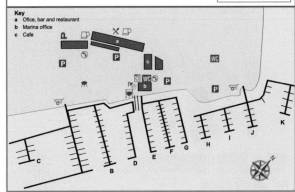

KEMPS QUAY

Kemp's Shipyard Ltd
Quayside Road, Southampton, SO18 1BZ
Tel: 023 8063 2323 Fax: 023 8022 6002
Email: enquiries@kempsquay.com

VHF
ACCESS HW±3.5

At the head of the River Itchen on the starboard side is Kemps Quay, a family-run marina with a friendly, old-fashioned feel. Accessible only 3½ hrs either side of HW, it has a limited number of deep water berths, the rest being half tide, drying out to soft mud. Its restricted access is, however, reflected in the lower prices.

Although situated on the outskirts of Southampton, a short bus or taxi ride will soon get you to the city centre. Besides a nearby BP Garage selling bread and milk, the closest supermarkets can be found in Bitterne Shopping Centre, which is five minutes away by bus.

FACILITIES AT A GLANCE

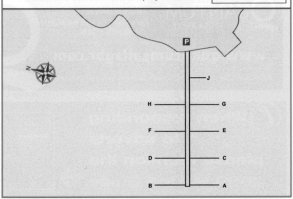

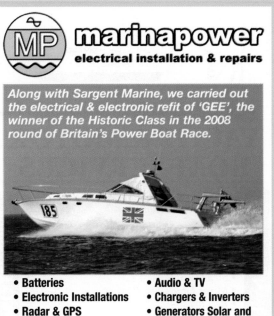

SAXON WHARF MARINA

Saxon Wharf Marina
Lower York Street, Northam
Southampton, SO14 5QF
Tel: 023 8033 9490 Fax: 023 8033 5215
www.marinas.co.uk Email: m.leigh@mdlmarinas.co.uk

| VHF | Ch 80 |
| ACCESS | H24 |

Saxon Wharf is a relatively new development which is situated towards the top of the River Itchen at the head of Southampton Water. Equipped with 50-metre marina berths and heavy duty pontoons, it is intended to accommodate superyachts and larger vessels. Boasting a 200-ton boat hoist and several marine specialists, including Southampton Yacht Services, it is the ideal place for the refit and restoration of big boats, whether it be a quick liftout or a large scale project. Located close to Southampton city centre and airport, Saxon Wharf is easily accessible by road, rail or air.

FACILITIES AT A GLANCE

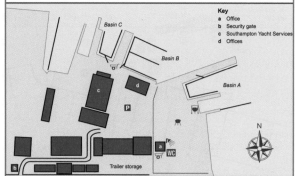

Key
a Office
b Security gate
c Southampton Yacht Services
d Offices

HAMBLE POINT MARINA

Hamble Point Marina
School Lane, Hamble, Southampton, SO31 4NB
Tel: 023 8045 2464 Fax: 023 8045 6440
Email: hamblepoint@mdlmarinas.co.uk

| VHF | Ch 80 |
| ACCESS | H24 |

Situated virtually opposite Warsash, this is the first marina you will come to on the western bank of the Hamble. Accommodating yachts up to 20m and power boats to 25m in length, it offers easy access to the Solent.
As with all the berths in the Hamble, be careful when manoeuvring at certain states of the tide and if possible try to avoid berthing when the tide is ebbing strongly. Boasting extensive facilities, the marina is within a 15-minute walk of Hamble Village, where services include a plethora of pubs and restaurants as well as a post office, bank and general store.

FACILITIES AT A GLANCE

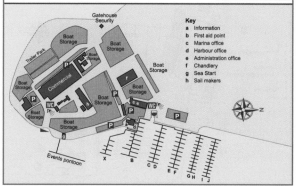

Key
a Information
b First aid point
c Marina office
d Harbour office
e Administration office
f Chandlery
g Sea Start
h Sail makers

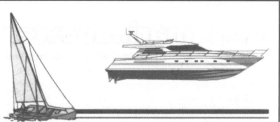

PORT HAMBLE MARINA

Port Hamble Marina
Satchell Lane, Hamble, Southampton, SO31 4QD
Tel: 023 8045 2741 Fax: 023 8045 5206
Email: porthamble@mdlmainas.co.uk www.marinas.co.uk

VHF | Ch 80
ACCESS | H24

On the west bank of the River Hamble, Port Hamble is the closest marina to the picturesque Hamble Village, therefore proving extremely popular with visiting yachtsmen. However, with no dedicated places for visitors, berthing availability is often scarce in the summer and it is best to contact the marina ahead of time.

Besides exploring the River Hamble, renowned for its maritime history which began as far back as the ninth century when King Alfred's men sank some 20 Viking long ships at Bursledon, other nearby places of interest include the 13th century Netley Abbey, allegedly haunted by Blind Peter the monk, and the Royal Victoria Country Park.

FACILITIES AT A GLANCE

Key
a Dock manager's office
b Boat sales
c Royal Air Force YC
d Hamble yacht services
e Bar/restaurant

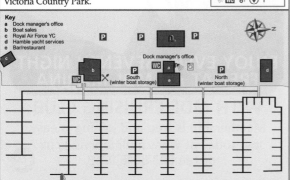

MERCURY YACHT HARBOUR

Mercury Yacht Harbour
Satchell Lane, Hamble, Southampton, SO31 4HQ
Tel: 023 8045 5994 Fax: 023 8045 7369
Email: mercury@mdlmarinas.co.uk www.marinas.co.uk

VHF | Ch 80
ACCESS | H24

Mercury Yacht Harbour is the third marina from seaward on the western bank of the River Hamble, tucked away in a picturesque, wooded site adjacent to Badnam Creek. Enjoying deep water at all states of the tide, it accommodates yachts up to 24m LOA and boasts an extensive array of facilities.

Hamble Village is at least a 20-minute walk away, although the on site chandlery does stock a small amount of essential items, and for a good meal you need look no further than the Oyster Quay bar and restaurant whose balcony offers striking of the water.

FACILITIES AT A GLANCE

Key
a Toilets and showers
b Launderette
c Chandlery
d Restaurant and bar
e Marine surveyor
f Dockmaster,
  marina manager's office
g Waste disposal
h Recycling area

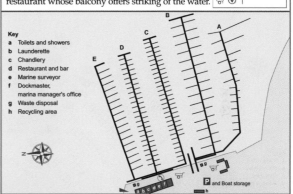

SWANWICK MARINA

Swanwick Marina
Swanwick, Southampton, Hampshire, SO31 1ZL
Tel: 01489 884081 Fax: 01489 579073
Email: swanwick@premiermarinas.com
www.premiermarinas.com

VHF	Ch 80
ACCESS	H24

Situated on the east bank of the River Hamble next to Bursledon Bridge, Swanwick Marina is accessible at all states of the tide and can accommodate yachts up to 20m LOA.

The marina's fully-licensed bar and bistro, Velshedas, overlooking the river, is open for breakfast, lunch and dinner during the summer. Alternatively, just a short row or walk away is the celebrated Jolly Sailor pub in Bursledon on the west bank, made famous for being the local watering hole in the British television series *Howard's Way*.

FACILITIES AT A GLANCE

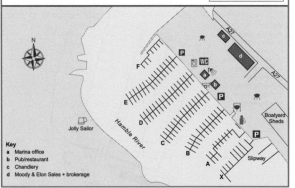

Key
a Marina office
b Pub/restaurant
c Chandlery
d Moody & Elon Sales + brokerage

RYDE LEISURE HARBOUR

Ryde Harbour
The Esplanade, Ryde, Isle of Wight, PO33 1JA
Tel: 01983 613879 Fax: 01983 613903
www.rydeharbour.com Email: ryde.harbour@iow.gov.uk

VHF	Ch 80
ACCESS	HW±2

Known as the 'gateway to the Island', Ryde, with its elegant houses and abundant shops, is among the Isle of Wight's most popular resorts. Its well-protected harbour is conveniently close to the exceptional beaches as well as to the town's restaurants and amusements.

Drying to 2.5m and therefore only accessible to yachts that can take the ground, the harbour accommodates 90 resident boats as well as up to 75 visiting yachts. Fin keel yachts may dry out on the harbour wall.

Ideal for family cruising, Ryde offers a wealth of activities, ranging from ten pin bowling and ice skating to crazy golf and tennis.

FACILITIES AT A GLANCE

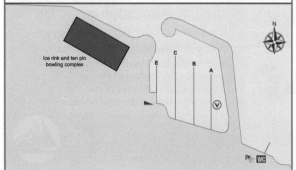

Ice rink and ten pin bowling complex

BEMBRIDGE MARINA

Bembridge Marina
Harbour Office, The Duver, St Helens, Ryde
Isle of Wight, PO33 1YB
Tel: 01983 872828 Fax: 01983 872922
Email: chris@bembridgeharbour.co.uk
www.bembridgeharbour.co.uk

VHF	Ch 80
ACCESS	HW±2.5

Bembridge is a compact, pretty harbour whose entrance, although restricted by the tides (recommended entry for a 1.5m draught is 2½hrs before HW), is well sheltered in all but north north easterly gales. Offering excellent sailing clubs, beautiful beaches and fine restaurants, this Isle of Wight port is a first class haven with plenty of charm. With approximately 100 new visitors' berths on the Duver Marina pontoons, the marina at St Helen's Quay, at the western end of the harbour, is now allocated to annual berth holders only.

FACILITIES AT A GLANCE

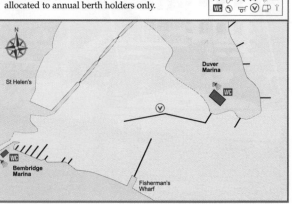

St Helen's

Duver Marina

Bembridge Marina

Fisherman's Wharf

HASLAR MARINA

Haslar Marina
Haslar Road, Gosport, Hampshire, PO12 1NU
Tel: 023 9260 1201 Fax: 023 9260 2201
www.haslarmarina.co.uk Email: sales@haslarmarina.co.uk

VHF | Ch 80
ACCESS | H24

This modern, purpose-built marina lies to port on the western side of Portsmouth Harbour entrance and is easily recognised by its prominent lightship incorporating a bar and restaurant. Accessible at all states of the tide, Haslar's extensive facilities do not however include fuel, the nearest being at the Camper and Nicholsons jetty only a few cables north.

Within close proximity is the Royal Navy Submarine Museum and the Museum of Naval Firepower 'Explosion' both worth a visit.

FACILITIES AT A GLANCE

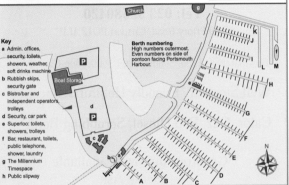

Key
a Admin. offices, security, toilets, showers, weather, soft drinks machine
b Rubbish skips, security gate
c Bistro/bar and independent operators, trolleys
d Security, car park
e Superloo: toilets, showers, trolleys
f Bar, restaurant, toilets, public telephone, shower, laundry
g The Millennium Timespace
h Public slipway

Berth numbering
High numbers outermost. Even numbers on side of pontoon facing Portsmouth Harbour.

ROYAL CLARENCE MARINA

Royal Clarence Marina, Royal Clarence Yard
Weevil Lane, Gosport, Hampshire PO12 1AX
Tel: 023 9252 3810 Fax: 023 9252 3980
Email: enquiries@royalclarencemarina.co.uk
www.royalclarencemarina.co.uk

VHF | Ch 80
ACCESS | H24

Royal Clarence Marina benefits from a unique setting within a deep-water basin in front of the Royal Navy's former victualling yard. Only 10 minutes from the entrance to Portsmouth Harbour, it forms part of a £100 million redevelopment scheme which will incorporate residential homes, waterfront bars and restaurants as well as shopping outlets. Among its facilities are fully serviced finger pontoon berths up to 18m in length, while over 200m of alongside berthing will accommodate Yacht Club rallies and other maritime events.

FACILITIES AT A GLANCE

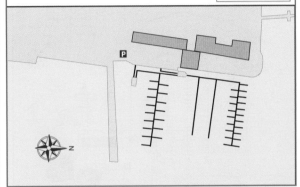

Bembridge Harbour

2009/MG13/e

Bembridge Harbour welcomes visiting yachts which are now accommodated at the new Duver Marina providing access to the shore on the north side of the harbour. Rafting will be necessary at busy times. Showers and toilets, formerly in the Marina Office, are now located on the old Duver Boatyard site.

Water Taxi
The Water Taxi operates a service to ferry visitors to other parts of the harbour where there are various pick-up points.

Reservations
Reservations are not accepted for visitors' berths which are allocated strictly on a first-come, first-served basis. Visitors should call VHF Channel 80 for berthing instructions before entering the harbour.

ASSURING YOU OF A WARM AND FRIENDLY WELCOME
Harbour Master: Chris Turvey
Bembridge Harbour Improvements Company Limited.
Harbour Office, The Duver, St Helens, Ryde, Isle of Wight, PO33 1YB
Tel: 01983 872828 · Fax: 01983 872922
email: chris@bembridgeharbour.co.uk
web: www.bembridgeharbour.co.uk

GOSPORT MARINA

Premier Gosport Marina
Mumby Road, Gosport, Hampshire, PO12 1AH
Tel: 023 9252 4811 Fax: 023 9258 9541
Email: gosport@premiermarinas.com
www.premiermarinas.com

VHF	Ch 80
ACCESS	H24

A few cables north of Haslar Marina, again on the port hand side, lies Gosport Marina. Boasting 519 fully-serviced visitors' berths, its extensive range of facilities incorporates a fuel barge on its southern breakwater as well as shower and laundry amenities. Numerous boatyard and engineering specialists are also located in and around the premises.

Within easy reach of the marina is Gosport town centre, offering a cosmopolitan selection of restaurants along with several supermarkets and shops.

FACILITIES AT A GLANCE

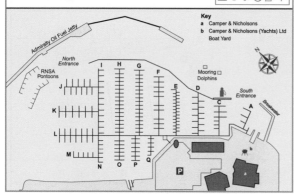

Key
a Camper & Nicholsons
b Camper & Nicholsons (Yachts) Ltd Boat Yard

PORT SOLENT MARINA

Port Solent Marina
South Lockside, Portsmouth, PO6 4TJ
Tel: 023 9221 0765 Fax: 023 9232 4241
www.premiermarinas.com
Email: portsolent@premiermarinas.com

VHF	Ch 80
ACCESS	H24

Port Solent Marina is located to the north east of Portsmouth Harbour, not far from the historic Portchester Castle. Accessible via a 24-hour lock, this purpose built

marina offers a full range of facilities. The Boardwalk comprises an array of shops and restaurants, while close by is a David Lloyd Health Centre and a large Odeon cinema.

No visit to Portsmouth Harbour is complete without a trip to the Historic Dockyard, home to Henry VIII's *Mary Rose*, Nelson's HMS *Victory* and the first iron battleship, HMS *Warrior*, built in 1860.

FACILITIES AT A GLANCE

Key
a Laundry, berth holders showers, toilets and baby change
b Portsmouth Harbour YC
c Chandlery, marine engineers
d Under cover boat shed
e Berth holders showers, toilets and public toilets, baby change
f David Lloyd Health and Fitness Club
g The Boardwalk - bars/restaurants
h Odeon cinema
I Marina control and Port Solent reception
J Residential building

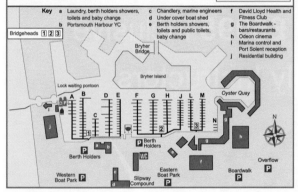

SOUTHSEA MARINA

Southsea Marina
Fort Cumberland Road, PO4 9RJ
Tel: 02392 822719 Fax: 02392 822220
Email: southsea@premiermarinas.com
www.premiermarinas.com

VHF	Ch 80
ACCESS	HW±3

Southsea Marina is a small and friendly marina located on the western shore of Langstone Harbour, an expansive tidal bay situated between Hayling Island and Portsmouth. The channel is clearly marked by seven starboard and nine port hand

markers. A tidal gate allows unrestricted movement in and out of the marina up to 3 hours either side of HW operates the entrance. The minimum depth in the marina entrance during this period is 1.6m and a waiting pontoon is available. There are excellent on site facilities including a bar, restaurant and chandlery.

FACILITIES AT A GLANCE

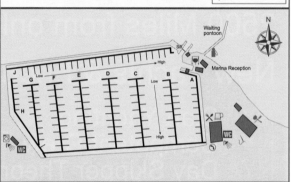

SPARKES YACHT HARBOUR

Sparkes Yacht Harbour
Wittering Road, Hayling Island, Hampshire, PO11 9SR
Tel: 023 9246 3572 Fax: 023 9246 5741
Email: info@sparkes.co.uk   www.sparkes.co.uk

VHF	Ch 80
ACCESS	H24

Just inside the entrance to Chichester Harbour, on the eastern shores of Hayling Island, lies Sparkes Marina and Boatyard. Its approach channel has been dredged to 2m MLW and can be identified by an unlit ECM. One of two marinas in

Chichester to have full tidal access, its facilities include a wide range of marine services as well as a well-stocked chandlery and first class restaurant. Within close proximity are a newsagent, farm shop and various takeaways, while a taxi ride away are Capers and Jaspers, two restaurants on Hayling Island renowned for their top quality cuisine.

FACILITIES AT A GLANCE

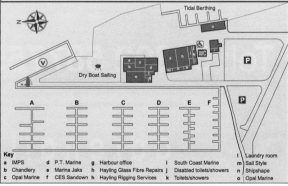

Key
a IMPS
b Chandlery
c Opal Marine
d P.T. Marine
e Marina Jaks
f CES Sandown
g Harbour office
h Hayling Glass Fibre Repairs
h Hayling Rigging Services
i South Coast Marine
j Disabled toilets/showers
k Toilets/showers
l Laundry room
m Sail Style
n Shipshape
o Opal Marine

2

PORT SOLENT MARINA
South Lockside, Port Solent, Portsmouth, Hampshire PO6 4TJ
Tel: (023) 9221 0765 Fax: (023) 9232 4241
e-mail: portsolent@premiermarinas.co.uk
www.permiermarinas.com
Situated in Portsmouth Harbour, Port Solent offers every facility a boatowner could wish for.
2009/L2c/z

SOUTHSEA MARINA
Fort Cumberland Marina, Portsmouth, Hampshire PO4 9RJ
Tel: (023) 9282 2719 Fax: (023) 9282 2220
e-mail: southsea@premiermarinas.co.uk
www.permiermarinas.com
A small and friendly Marina on the doorstep of the Solent.
2009/L2d/z

NORTHNEY MARINA

Northney Marina
Northney Road, Hayling Island, Hampshire, PO11 0NH
Tel: 023 9246 6321 Fax: 023 9246 1467
www.marinas.co.uk Email: northney@mdlmarinas.co.uk

VHF Ch 80
ACCESS H24

One of two marinas in Chichester Harbour to be accessible at all states of the tide, Northney Marina is on the northern shore of Hayling Island in the well marked Sweare Deep Channel, which branches off to port almost at the end of the Emsworth Channel. With a new facilities block having recently been completed, the marina now incorporates a very basic grocery store as well as improved ablution facilities. There is an events area for rallies.

FACILITIES AT A GLANCE

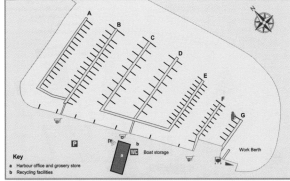

Key
a Harbour office and grocery store
b Recycling facilities

EMSWORTH YACHT HARBOUR

Emsworth Yacht Harbour
Thorney Road, Emsworth, Hants, PO10 8BP
Tel: 01243 377727 Fax: 01243 373432
Email: info@emsworth-marina.co.uk
www.emsworth-marina.co.uk

VHF | Ch 80
ACCESS | HW±2

Accessible about one and a half to two hours either side of high water, Emsworth Yacht Harbour is a sheltered site, offering good facilities to yachtsmen.

Created in 1964 from a log pond, the marina is within easy walking distance of the pretty little town of Emsworth, which boasts at least 10 pubs, several high quality restaurants and two well-stocked convenience stores.

FACILITIES AT A GLANCE

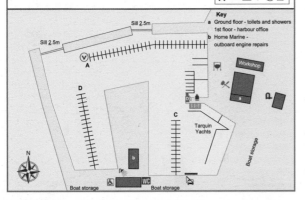

Key
a Ground floor - toilets and showers
  1st floor - harbour office
b Home Marine - outboard engine repairs

CHICHESTER MARINA

Chichester Marina
Birdham, Chichester, West Sussex, PO20 7EJ
Tel: 01243 512731 Fax: 01243 513472
Email: chichester@premiermarinas.com
www.premiermarinas.com

VHF | Ch 80
ACCESS | HW±5

Chichester Marina, nestling in an enormous natural harbour, has more than 1,000 berths, making it one of the largest marinas in the UK. Its approach channel can be easily identified by the CM SHM pile. The channel was dredged to 0.5m below CD in 2004, giving access of around five hours either side of HW at springs. Besides the wide ranging marine facilities, there are also a restaurant and small convenience store on site. Chichester, which is only about a five minute bus or taxi ride away, has several places of interest, the most notable being the cathedral.

FACILITIES AT A GLANCE

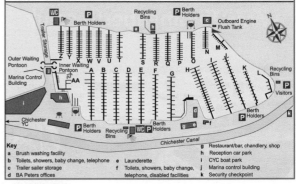

Key
a Brush washing facility
b Toilets, showers, baby change, telephone
c Trailer sailer storage
d BA Peters offices
e Launderette
f Toilets, showers, baby change, telephone, disabled facilities
g Restaurant/bar, chandlery, shop
h Reception car park
i CYC boat park
j Marina control building
k Security checkpoint

BIRDHAM POOL MARINA

Birdham Pool Marina
Birdham Pool, Chichester, Sussex
Tel: 01243 512310 Fax: 01243 513163
Email: info@birdhampool.co.uk

VHF | Ch 80
ACCESS | HW±3

Birdham Pool must be among Britain's most charming and rustic marinas. Only accessible three hours either side of HW via a lock, any visiting yachtsman will not be disappointed by its unique and picturesque setting. To get to Birdham Pool, enter the channel at the Birdham SHM beacon. The channel is marked by green piles that should be left no more than 3m to starboard. There is a wide range of marine facilities on hand, including a small chandlery that opens six days a week.

FACILITIES AT A GLANCE

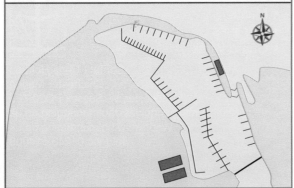